Chicago Public Library
W9-AFT-916
Barry Bonds

Barry Bonds

by Raymond H. Miller

KIDHAVEN PRESS™

THOMSON GALE™

San Diego • Detroit • New York • San Francisco • Cleveland
New Haven, Conn. • Waterville, Maine • London • Munich

For more information, contact
KidHaven Press
27500 Drake Rd.
Farmington Hills, MI 48331-3535
Or you can visit our Internet site at http://www.gale.com

LIBRARY OF CONGRESS CATALOGING-IN-PUBLICATION DATA

Miller, Raymond H., 1967–
Barry Bonds / by Raymond H. Miller
p. cm.—(Stars of sports)
Includes bibliographical references.
Summary: Discusses the personality, marriage, baseball career, and home run legacy of Barry Bonds.
ISBN 0-7377-1393-3 (hard : alk. paper)
1.Bonds, Barry, 1964– Juvenile literature. 2. Baseball players—United States—Biography—Juvenile literature. [1. Bonds, Barry, 1964– 2. Baseball players. 3. African Americans—biography.] I. Title. II. Series.
GV865 .B637 M55 2003
796.357'092—dc21

2002003276

Printed in the United States of America

Contents

Introduction

The Complete Player

In 2001 Barry Bonds broke Major League Baseball's single-season home run record. He also became the sport's first four-time Most Valuable Player (MVP), establishing himself as one of the greatest players in the history of the game. He is a superb athlete with a unique combination of skills. He hits for power, runs the bases with a burst of speed, and is nearly flawless in the outfield. Baseball experts call him the complete player.

Even though Bonds has made it to the top of the baseball world and is destined for the Hall of Fame, stardom did not come easy. Early in his career he struggled with the pressure of being the son of a big league star. He finally stepped out of his father's shadow when he led the Pittsburgh Pirates to three straight division titles in the early 1990s. And when he joined the San Francisco Giants in 1993, he turned a last-place team into a winner.

Through the years, Bonds has won numerous batting and fielding awards. He is rapidly climbing the all-time home run list and might someday make it to the top. But one goal he has never achieved at any level—high school, college, or the pros—is winning a championship. For all that he has accomplished, he will not be satisfied until his team is crowned World Series champion.

Barry Bonds hits a home run for the Pittsburgh Pirates, leading them to a division title in 1990.

Chapter One

Born into Baseball

Barry Lamar Bonds was born to play baseball. His father, Bobby, was an all-star outfielder who played for the San Francisco Giants and several other Major League Baseball teams. Barry's mother, Patricia, is a cousin of baseball great Reggie Jackson. And Barry's godfather is Willie Mays, Bobby's teammate with the Giants and one of the most famous players of all time.

Born on July 24, 1964, in Riverside, California, Barry grew up near San Francisco with two younger brothers, Ricky and Bobby Jr., and a younger sister, Cheryl. Baseball was a big part of Barry's young life, even before he was old enough to know it. At age two, Barry picked up a baseball bat and began swinging it. Even at that young age, he could hit a ball. He once smacked a Whiffle ball

From left to right, Willie Mays, Bobby Bonds, Andre Dawson, and Barry Bonds pose for the 300 Home Runs/ 300 Stolen Bases Club photo in 1996.

so hard it broke a window. After that, no window was safe when Barry had a bat in his hands. Patricia joked that she was a regular customer at the local glass store because of Barry's powerful hits.

When Barry was a few years older, his mother took him to nearby Candlestick Park (now called 3Com Park) to watch his father play for the Giants. Bobby was Barry's favorite player. He also loved watching Mays play center field. Before the games, Barry put on a miniature Giants uniform and ran around the outfield pretending to be a real player. He was too young to take batting practice, but he showed a knack for catching fly balls.

Bobby Bonds shakes his teammates' hands as he crosses home plate after hitting a three-run homer in 1968.

Growing up around the game and spending time at a professional ballpark gave Barry a jump-start in baseball. He could catch better, run faster, and hit the ball farther than most kids his age.

An Early Start

When Barry was seven years old, he joined other kids on a **farm league** baseball team. Farm league was an instructional league below Little League. He had already been taught by some of the game's best players, so he stood out on the diamond early on. In one farm league game, he hit a ball that sailed over the outfielders' heads and rolled all the way to the fence. He sprinted around the bases for a game-winning home run. Barry found himself in the baseball spotlight for the first time, and he loved it. He later said that game-winning homer was the start of his baseball career.

Because his father was on the road with the Giants a lot of the time, Barry practiced for hours with his mother. The two became very close. His mother went to most of his games and stood in for his dad at many school events. Barry later recalled how important his mother was to him (and to his brothers and sister). "She did everything for us," he said. "She always took me to baseball or football

Barry Bonds kisses his mother Patricia after hitting his five hundredth home run.

practice. She always wrote 'from Dad' on the Christmas presents. My mom was at all the school events. My dad never went. He was playing baseball."[1]

By the time Barry entered high school, everyone knew who he was because of his famous last name. While some kids his age enjoyed being the center of attention, Barry did not. His baseball teammates teased him by calling him "Bobby" when he got a base hit. They said the only reason he was any good was because of his father. Barry was hurt and angered by the comments. At times, Barry made the situation worse for himself by being moody or unfriendly.

Three-Sport Star

In the classroom, Barry was an average student who studied just enough to get by. His eleventh grade biology teacher, frustrated at Barry's lack of effort, tried to motivate him to study harder and take school more seriously. The teacher warned him not to depend on a baseball career later in life, because few people made it to the professional level. Barry did not listen. He continued to favor baseball, basketball, and football over his studies.

Baseball was his best sport, and his favorite. He led his high school team to the section championship his sophomore, junior, and senior seasons. His **batting average** was .467 as a senior, which made him a prep all-American. This award is given to the nation's best high school sports players.

Barry's success on the ball field, and his name, got the attention of college and professional baseball **scouts**. The

San Francisco Giants team was so impressed that in 1982, right after his high school graduation, it drafted Barry in the second round. The Giants offered him a $70,000 signing bonus, but his father did not think it was enough money. Barry turned down the Giants and decided instead to play baseball in college. Arizona State University wanted him, and it offered him a full **scholarship**, which he accepted. He left home in the fall of 1982 and headed to Tempe, Arizona, to begin the next step in his baseball career.

Barry Bonds in his senior yearbook picture. As a senior, Bonds was named one of the nation's best high school baseball players.

Sun Devil Days

Barry's teammates on the Arizona State Sun Devils quickly saw why the Giants had drafted him out of high school. He ran the forty-yard dash in an amazing 4.3 seconds and had a smooth, powerful swing. He hit balls with topspin over the fence for home runs. When other batters hit balls with topspin, their balls landed short of the fence. His strength surprised people because he was tall and lacked the muscles of a typical power hitter.

Off the field, Barry struggled to fit in. Although he sometimes hung around with teammates in the dugout, for the most part Barry was a private person who did not seem to get along with the other players. At times, he bragged about how much money he turned down from the Giants, or boasted about his father's accomplishments. Other times he acted as though he was above the rules. When the Sun Devils were in Hawaii for a game, for example, he and a few of his teammates stayed out

Bonds's Arizona State University Baseball Statistics

Year	At Bat	Runs	Hits	Home Runs	Runs Batted In	Stolen Bases	Batting Average
1983	206	60	63	11	54	16	.306
1984	258	62	93	11	55	30	.360
1985	247	61	91	23	66	11	.368
Totals	711	183	247	45	175	57	.347

Barry Bonds ASU Facts

- Member of the all-College World Series team in 1983 and 1984.
- Member of the all-Pac-10 Conference in 1984 and 1985.
- MVP of the 1983 West II Regional Tournament at ASU.
- All-America selection by Baseball America in 1985.
- Bonds's eleven home runs in 1983 remain an ASU Freshman record.
- Achieved fifty-four RBI during his freshman season.

past curfew. The next day, as punishment, the coach ordered them to run ten miles. Barry was the only one to complain and was nearly suspended from the team.

Although Barry had a lot to learn off the field, on the field his talents shone. In one game, he hit two line drive home runs to left field. Everyone who saw the hitting display was amazed because few college players had the strength to hit line drives over the opposite field fence. Barry was definitely not a typical player. In three seasons at Arizona State, he hit forty-five home runs and had an outstanding .347 batting average. He also helped lead the Sun Devils to two College World Series (CWS) playoff appearances. As a sophomore, Barry set a CWS record with seven straight hits. But his team lost in the series that year and the next.

By 1985, when Barry was still a junior in college, he decided he was ready to turn pro. The Pittsburgh Pirates selected him with the sixth pick in the first round of the draft. Baseball experts believed he should have been the first player picked overall, but many teams had concerns about his attitude. The Pirates were not one of those teams. They were convinced he was the best player in the draft, and they signed him to a four-year contract. He was twenty years old.

Chapter Two

Pride of the Pirates

Bonds was one of the top college players in the nation in 1985, but the Pirates did not believe he had enough experience to play at the major league level right away. They sent him to the **minor leagues** to train. Each professional team has at least four minor league teams: Triple-A (the highest level), Double-A, Single-A, and rookie league (the lowest level). He started out with Pittsburgh's Single-A team in Virginia—the Prince William Pirates.

In seventy-one games at Prince William, Bonds had a .299 batting average with thirteen home runs and thirty-seven runs batted in (RBI). The coaches were so impressed that they moved him up to their Triple-A team in Honolulu, Hawaii, to start the 1986 season. After batting .311 in forty-four games in Triple-A, he was ready to join the team in Pittsburgh.

Bobby Bonds's Son

The Pirates were a team in **disarray** when Bonds arrived in Pittsburgh in May 1986. The owners had considered moving the team to another city because they were losing money from low fan attendance. To make matters worse, the Pirates were off to a poor start and were in last place. With Bonds on the team, more and more fans came to the stadium. They had heard about him from the minor leagues and wanted to watch him play in person. In his second game, he collected his first career

Bonds drives a fastball into the air for a double against the Los Angeles Dodgers.

hit—a double—against the Los Angeles Dodgers. A few days later he hit his first major league home run against the Atlanta Braves. He celebrated the occasion by ordering pizza for the whole team after the game. The young rookie was eager to fit in with his new teammates.

As the son of a famous ballplayer, people often compared the two. Barry looked and played like a young Bobby Bonds, often displaying the same rare combination of speed and power. Reporters sometimes called him "Bobby" by mistake. But he did not like being compared to anyone else, even his father. The only way to end the comparisons was to become a better ball player than his father.

Stardom did not come to Bonds in his first year with Pittsburgh. He batted just .223 and struck out more than one hundred times. He summed up his first season in the major leagues by saying, "I'm 22 years old and still trying to find out the type of player I am going to be in this game. But I'm not so concerned about my own individual self as I am about my team winning."[2] The Pirates did not win that season, finishing with the worst record in baseball. But the team had a group of young players with bright futures, and Bonds showed the most promise of all.

Mr. MVP

Bonds's personal life took an unexpected turn in 1987 when he met and fell in love with a young Swedish woman named Sunsann "Sun" Margreth. The two dated for several months, then married in February 1988. He and Sun later had two children, Nikolai and Shakira.

Number 24, Barry Bonds, jumps to catch a fly ball in front of the L.A. Dodgers dugout.

Bonds's career also underwent some changes. He moved from center field to left field when the Pirates acquired a new center fielder. He also swapped uniform numbers. He wore number seven during his rookie season, but in his second season he chose number twenty-four—his high school and college number. Bonds was thrilled to be wearing the same number as his idol (and godfather), Willie Mays. The new number suited him well as he raised his batting average to .261. The next season, his average climbed even higher and the Pirates showed definite improvement. He did not perform well offensively in 1989, but he won his first **Gold Glove Award**. The award is given to players who are chosen by coaches and managers as the best at their defensive positions.

When the season ended, Bonds spent many hours lifting weights, jogging, and hitting in the batting cage. His hard work paid off when he batted .302 in 1990. He joined baseball's exclusive 30-30 club by hitting more than thirty home runs and stealing more than thirty bases that season. He was named Most Valuable Player of the National League. In 1992 he won the award again after having career highs in batting average (.311) and home runs (thirty-four). When he was presented with the award, he dedicated it to his mother because of everything she had done for him. He had finally made a name for himself.

Charming and Distant

Stardom seemed to change Bonds's relationship with the press. Earlier in his career, he gave interviews almost whenever he was asked. But as his fame grew, reporters began writing that he was moody, and not always a team player. Soon, he began to dislike talking to reporters and sometimes ignored them altogether. He once made a writer from *Sports Illustrated* wait four days to interview him. Reporters never knew how he was going to act. He could be charming and friendly one day, and cold and

As a Pirate, Bonds won his first Gold Glove Award and two MVP's for the National League.

Bonds, waving off a cameraman, often refused interviews with the news media.

distant the next. For the most part, he just wanted to be left alone to play the game he loved.

Fall Fizzle

Bonds's outstanding play turned the Pirates into winners. In 1990 the team won the National League Eastern Division for the first time in eleven years. The Pirates won their division again in 1991 and met the Atlanta Braves in the National League Championship Series (NLCS). But Bonds was stuck in a batting slump and was unable to make an impact at the plate. In seven games, he did not hit a home run or drive in a run. The

Braves beat the Pirates and headed to the World Series. The press blamed Bonds for the series loss, even though some of his teammates did not play well either. He thought the **criticism** was unfair and it damaged his rocky relationship with the press even more.

The next year Bonds led the Pirates to their third straight division title, and once again the Pirates played the Braves in the NLCS. After losing games one and two, the team rallied to win three of the next four. With the series tied at three games apiece, the Pirates had a 2-1 lead and were one out away from the World Series. The Braves loaded the bases and the next Atlanta batter dropped a base hit into left field. One runner scored to tie the game. Bonds raced to the ball and made a great throw to the plate, but it was a split-second too late. The second runner scored and the Pirates lost the game 3-2. Bonds sat in front of his locker after the game and did not say a word. Although he had played much better in that series than he had in the first two, he was heartbroken.

Free Agent

It was a sad ending to Bonds's career in Pittsburgh. He was a **free agent** that winter, meaning he could sign a contract to play for any other team in the league. Pirates management could not afford to pay him what he deserved, and his coach told him it was time to move on. So he left Pittsburgh to begin his search for another ball club. He informed the media that he wanted to play for any of the California teams, except one. Surprisingly, the one team not on his list was the San Francisco Giants.

Chapter Three

A Giant Star

Bonds's reason for not wanting to return to his hometown was its chilly weather. Night games at Candlestick Park were often cold, windy, and foggy, which made it hard to hit home runs. And catching fly balls in the wind and fog was tricky for outfielders, even for a Gold Glove Award winner like Bonds. He wanted to play in a warm-weather city where he could hit plenty of home runs.

Giants management knew Bonds wanted to play elsewhere, but they made an offer to him anyway. They presented him with the highest contract offer in baseball history: nearly $44 million over six years. Then the Giants told him his father would be hired as hitting instructor if he signed with the team. Barry was thrilled at the chance to finally spend time with his father. After talking to his family, he accepted the offer. He was headed home to play on the field where his father and godfather had played.

Fans in San Francisco were excited about a turnaround. The team finished in last place the previous year. Bonds had turned the Pirates into a winning ball club. San Franciscans hoped he could do that and more with the Giants. They wanted a World Series championship.

Candlestick Park, now known as 3Com Park, was home to Barry Bonds and the San Francisco Giants until 1999.

The Bonds Squad

In 1993 the Giants already had a team of established stars. Although Bonds's teammates were excited about the chance to win with him, it was not an easy time for some of them. Since 1986 Will Clark had been the team's most popular player and leader. When Bonds joined the team, he became the team's new leader because of his superstar status. But being a leader did not come naturally to him. He was not outspoken like Clark, nor was he as popular in the clubhouse.

Bonds did little to win over his new teammates. In one team meeting, he pointed out the Giants pitchers against whom he had hit home runs when he was playing for the Pirates. He was only showing his confident side, but some of the players did not appreciate a newcomer making them look bad. He already had a reputation for being somewhat **arrogant**, and his actions did not win him many friends in the clubhouse.

Bonds had no problem making friends in other places. He became involved in a charity called Adopt a Special Kid (AASK), an organization that places special-needs children into loving homes. Every time he hit a home run, drove in a run, or stole a base, he donated $100 to the charity. He also bought a large block of seats in the outfield at Candlestick Park for the AASK children. The section was called "The Bonds Squad."

When Bonds hit a home run over The Bonds Squad banner in his first at-bat as a Giant, fans leaped off their seats and celebrated. He stayed hot at the plate in April and was named Player of the Month by Major League

San Francisco Giants first baseman, Will Clark, was considered the team leader until Bonds arrived in 1993.

The Bonds Squad enjoys a day at the ballpark.

Baseball. For the next several months, he almost single-handedly kept the Giants in first place. Then he slumped in the second half of the season and the team lost eight straight games, allowing the Atlanta Braves to move into first place. With less than a month left in the 1993 season, he broke out of his slump and carried the team back toward the top. The Giants ended up with more than one hundred wins that year, but narrowly missed the playoffs. The unhappy ending did not spoil Bonds's season. After leading the league with 46 home runs and 123 RBI, he was named MVP for the third time in four years.

Tough Times

When the 1994 season began, Bonds picked up where he left off the year before. He was on pace to smash his home run total from the year before, when the season suddenly ended. The players union decided to strike, and the season and the World Series were canceled.

Major League Baseball players, eating in their locker room while a news broadcast announces the 1994 players' strike.

Bonds's personal life also went through a rough period. After six years of marriage, he and Sun divorced. The two had a long, bitter fight over how to divide their money and property, and the case ended up in court. The case attracted a lot of interest from the media. Many stories about his divorce appeared in newspapers and on television. In the end, the court sided with Barry, but he was unhappy about having his personal life discussed in public.

Bonds's messy breakup with his wife was the most difficult time in his life, and he seriously considered walking away from baseball. He let his feelings be known when he said, "All the newspapers think I'm this crazy, lunatic dude. Everywhere I go, people think I'm this, people think I'm that. But they don't even know the truth."[3]

Player of the 1990s

Bonds put his tough times behind him and by age thirty was considered the best all-around player in baseball. No one could match his hitting and fielding abilities or his speed running the bases. In 1996 he had forty-two home runs and forty stolen bases for the first 40-40 season of his career. Two years later he recorded his fifth 30-30 season, tying his father's major league record. He also became the first player in history to hit four hundred home runs and steal four hundred bases in a career.

The Giants were in the playoff race late in the 1997 season when Bonds took his game to a new level. He hit seven home runs in ten games to push his team into the

Bonds stands alert in the outfield in front of a sign celebrating his achievement of passing the forty home runs and forty stolen bases mark in 1996.

playoffs. But once they started, he repeated his postseason performances of the past. He had only three base hits and the Giants lost three straight games to the Florida Marlins. After the series loss, fans and reporters questioned why Bonds, a three-time MVP, always seemed to go cold in the postseason. He had a career .200 batting average with only one home run and five RBI in twenty-three playoff games. His postseason frustration surfaced

Bonds cheers from atop the Giants' dugout after beating the San Diego Padres to win the National League Western title in 1997.

during an interview when he said, "There are plenty of times when I can't take the abuse anymore. You're blamed for this, or you're blamed for that. That is a lonely place to be."[4]

As the 1990s came to an end, *Sporting News* named Bonds the Player of the Decade. From 1990 to 1999, his batting average was .302 with 361 home runs, 1,076 RBI, and 343 stolen bases. He surpassed his father's accomplishments and rose to the level of his godfather, Willie Mays.

Chapter Four

Home Run King

People started noticing a change in Bonds around the year 2000. He had married his childhood friend Liz Watson in 1998, and he was happier than ever. The two later had a daughter, Aisha Lynn. He told people that Liz was the best thing that ever happened to him. He said that some of the greatest years of his professional career took place after the two were married.

The players also noticed a difference in Bonds's personality. For example, during batting practice he gave them hitting tips, which he had not done before. And after hitting home runs in games, he pointed to his family in the stands and kissed his son, Nikolai, who was a batboy for the Giants. He also made an effort to be friendlier toward fans and the media. During postgame

Aisha Lynn shares a laugh with her father at a press conference after he broke the single-season home run record with seventy-one homers.

interviews, he often sat Aisha Lynn on his lap and answered questions from the press, sometimes letting his daughter talk into the microphone. He seemed to be showing the world a warmer, friendlier side of himself.

Although Bonds's relationship with his teammates had improved, some conflict remained. For example, for two years in a row, Bonds refused to pose for the team photograph. This angered his teammates. Second baseman Jeff Kent accused Bonds of not caring about his teammates, and the controversy seemed to spark a rivalry between the two players. In 2000 Bonds led the team with 49 home runs, a career high. Kent batted .334, drove in 125 runs, and was voted the league's MVP. Bonds finished second in the voting.

The two players led the Giants into the postseason against the New York Mets. After playing poorly in four

The New York Mets celebrate a victory over the Giants, clinching the National League Division title in 2000.

previous trips to the playoffs, Bonds put a lot of pressure on himself, and so did the media. But he batted just .176 with one RBI and failed to hit any home runs. The Giants lost the series to the Mets. Once again, he faced harsh criticism from the press. With the help of his family, he quickly put the playoff disappointment behind him and prepared for the next season.

Going . . . Going . . . Gone

Bonds started the 2001 season with a bang by hitting a home run on opening day. A few weeks later, he reached a baseball milestone when he hit his five hundredth career home run, something only sixteen other players in Major League Baseball had ever done. Later that season, he hit a remarkable twenty-one home runs in twenty-six games, and he was on pace to break the single-season home run record. Mark McGwire set the record in 1998 when he hit seventy home runs. Bonds insisted he did not care about breaking the record. He wanted something else—a World Series victory. "I just want to win and let everything happen on its own," he said. "I don't want to get too high on anything or too low. I've got a lot of individual accomplishments. I've done a lot in this game. But I've never won [a championship]. And it's important—it's really important."[5]

By the all-star break, Bonds had thirty-nine home runs and the Giants were playing well. In the second half of the season, he continued hitting home runs at a record pace and the team kept winning. He had sixty-three home runs when terrorists struck the United

Pressing his hands in wet cement, Bonds solidifies his place as one of the Giants' all-time best sluggers.

States on September 11, 2001. Bonds wanted to do something special for the people affected by the tragedy, so he decided to donate $10,000 to the United Way Relief Fund for every home run he hit the rest of the year.

When the season resumed, Bonds started hitting home runs again. With one week left in the season, he was one home run shy of tying the record. Pitchers purposely threw bad pitches to avoid giving up a home run. In a three-game series against the Houston Astros, the pitchers walked him eight times. But on October 4, in his last at-bat against the Astros, he finally got a good pitch to hit. He knocked it into the second outfield deck to tie the home run record. His teammates rushed to home plate to hug him. He was happy and relieved at the same time, but he still had work to do. There were only three games left to break the record.

The next night, October 5, in a home game against the Los Angeles Dodgers, Bonds hit a towering fly ball to deep right-center field. The sellout crowd at Pacific Bell Park leaped for joy as the ball cleared the fence for home run number seventy-one and the record. He was not finished that night. In a later at-bat, he hit another home run to break his own record. But in the end, it was not enough. The Giants lost the game 11-10 and were eliminated from the playoffs. After the game, he spoke to the fans about his historic achievement and thanked them for their support. His hero Willie Mays stood with him at the podium. When fans began chanting Bonds's name, he became so emotional that he broke down and cried.

Two days later, in the final game of the season, he hit his seventy-third home run to raise the record even higher. His contract with the Giants ended after the season and he was again free to sign with another team. He mentioned the possibility of playing in New York for either the Yankees or the Mets, or in Atlanta with the

Surrounded by his teammates, Barry Bonds picks up his son Nikolai after knocking his seventy-first home run in the 2001 season.

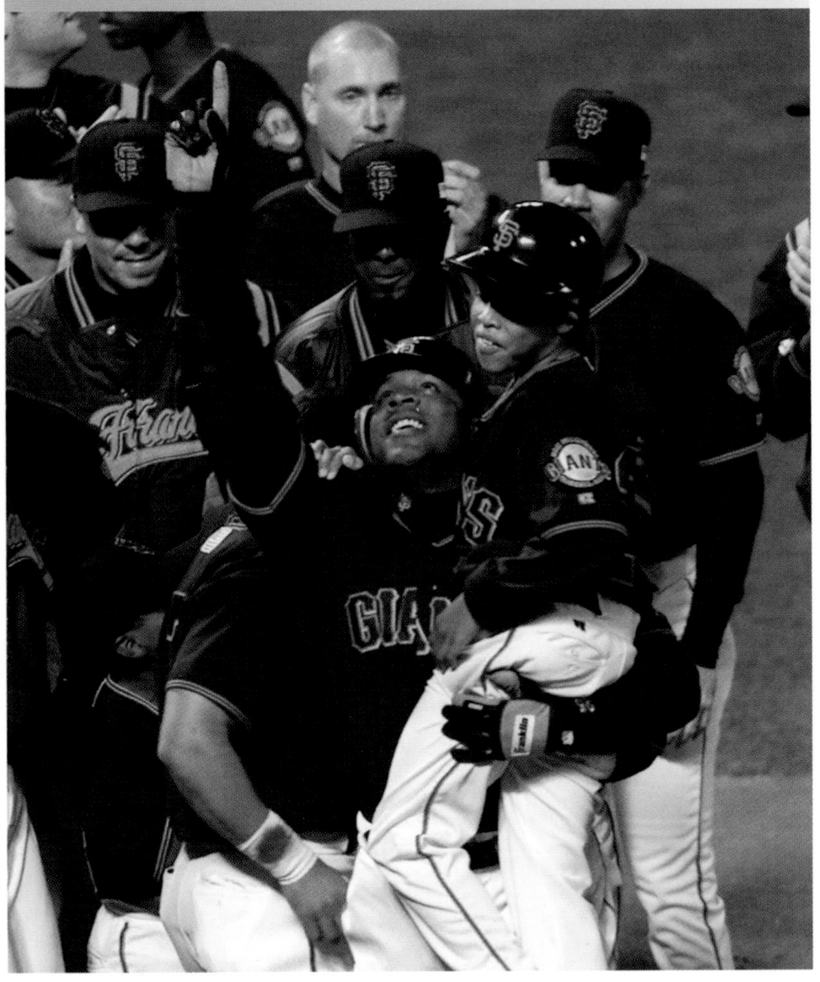

Bonds's Major League Baseball Statistics

Year	At Bat	Runs	Hits	Home Runs	Runs Batted In	Stolen Bases	Batting Average
1986	413	72	92	16	48	36	.223
1987	551	99	144	25	59	32	.261
1988	538	97	152	24	58	17	.283
1989	580	96	144	19	58	32	.248
1990	519	104	156	33	114	52	.301
1991	510	95	149	25	116	43	.292
1992	473	109	147	34	103	39	.311
1993	539	129	181	46	123	29	.336
1994	391	89	122	37	81	29	.312
1995	506	109	149	33	104	31	.294
1996	517	122	159	42	129	40	.308
1997	532	123	155	40	101	37	.291
1998	552	120	167	37	122	28	.303
1999	355	91	93	34	83	15	.262
2000	480	129	147	49	106	11	.306
2001	476	129	156	73	137	13	.328

Braves. But Giants management wanted to make sure Bonds remained in San Francisco for the rest of his career, so they signed him to a long-term contract. He was happy to be staying home.

Babe, Mickey, Willie . . . and Barry

In 2001 Bonds not only surpassed Mark McGwire's seemingly unbreakable home run record, but he also finished with a .328 batting average and a career-high 137 RBI. He was named the league's MVP, becoming the first player in baseball history to accomplish the feat four

Bonds holds the 2001 MVP trophy, making him the first baseball player to accomplish the feat four times.

times. This instantly put Bonds in select company. His name has been mentioned with those of baseball's greatest players, including Babe Ruth, Mickey Mantle, and Willie Mays.

Bonds has entered the final years of his brilliant career. He is a ten-time all-star, an eight-time Gold Glove Award winner, and the greatest single-season home run hitter in history. But individual achievements and awards are no longer what satisfy him. "The best of times for Barry Bonds will come when I've reached the promised land of the World Series and I can hold up my hand with a [championship] ring on my finger," he said. "That will be all the gratification and satisfaction I need."[6]

Notes

Chapter One: Born into Baseball

1. Quoted in Jeff Savage, *Barry Bonds: Mr. Excitement*, Minneapolis, MN: Lerner, 1997, p. 18.

Chapter Two: Pride of the Pirates

2. Quoted in Jeff Savage, *Barry Bonds: Mr. Excitement*, Minneapolis: Lerner Publications, 1997, p. 31

Chapter Three: A Giant Star

3. Barry Bonds, *ESPN SportsCentury*, "Barry Bonds," ESPN, 2001.
4. Bonds, *ESPN SportsCentury*.

Chapter Four: Home Run King

5. Quoted in Jon Saraceno, "Bonds' Glowing Statistics Truly Worth Appreciation," *USA Today*, October 2, 2001.
6. Quoted in Ross Newhan, "Postseason Success, Not Home Run Record Important to Bonds" *Los Angeles Times*, August 23, 2001.

Glossary

arrogant: Boastful or overly proud of oneself.

batting average: The average number of times a batter gets a base hit compared to the number of at-bats; base hits divided by at-bats (example: three hits in ten at-bats equals a .300 batting average).

criticism: Unfavorable remarks about a person.

disarray: A state of confusion or disorder.

farm league: An instructional baseball league for children aged seven and eight.

free agent: A professional player who is not under contract and is free to sign with another team.

Gold Glove Award: An award given to the best defensive player at each position.

minor leagues: A level of baseball that prepares players for the major leagues.

scholarship: A grant of money given to pay a college student's tuition.

scouts: People who evaluate talent.

For Further Exploration

Books

Larry Ekin, *Baseball Fathers, Baseball Sons*. Cincinnati: Betterway Books, 1992. Examines the baseball careers of famous father-son combinations, including Bobby Bonds and Barry Bonds, Ken Griffey Sr. and Ken Griffey Jr., and Cal Ripken Sr. and Cal Ripken Jr.

Michael E. Goodman, *Ovations: Barry Bonds*. Mankato, MN: Creative Education, 1998. A photograph-filled book that charts Barry Bonds's rise to the top of the baseball world. Includes a section of quotes from Bonds and the people closest to him.

Miles Harvey, *Barry Bonds: Baseball's Complete Player*. Chicago: Childrens Press, 1994. Tells the story of the life and career of Major League Baseball's best all-around player.

Carrie Muskat, *Barry Bonds*, Philadelphia: Chelsea House, 1997. A biography of the San Francisco Giants outfielder who rose to fame in the 1990s.

Jeff Savage, *Barry Bonds: Mr. Excitement*. Minneapolis: Lerner Publications, 1997. Takes a season-by-season glance at the baseball superstar's career, from his pre–Little League days to the Major League.

Websites

Barry Bonds Statistics: Baseball-Reference.com (http://baseball-reference.com). Keeps complete batting and fielding statistics on Barry Bonds. Also lists his awards, postseason statistics, All-Star appearances, and Most Valuable Player rankings.

ESPN.com: Barry Bonds (http://sports.espn.go.com). An excellent resource for up-to-date statistics on Barry Bonds. Also includes his career statistics, game logs, a hit chart, and more.

The Official Site of the San Francisco Giants (http://sanfrancisco.giants.mlb.com). The website has news articles, player profiles, team history, and other information about the San Francisco Giants.

Index

Picture Credits

Cover Photo: Associated Press, AP
© AFP/CORBIS, 32
Associated Press, AP, 7, 9, 17, 20, 29, 30, 33, 35
© Bettmann/CORBIS, 5, 8
© Stephen Dunn/Allsport, 15
© Otto Greule/Allsport, 26
© Jed Jacobson/Allsport, 23, 25, 27
Brandy Noon, 12, 19, 38
© Reuters NewMedia Inc./CORBIS, 37
YearbookArchives.com, 11

About the Author

Raymond H. Miller is the author of more than fifty nonfiction books for children. He has written on a range of topics, from sports trivia to fossilized shark teeth. A former college baseball player, he enjoys playing sports and spending time outdoors with his wife and daughters.